KURT ANGLE

FROM OLYMPIAN TO WRESTLING MACHINE

by Jason Skog

Consultant:
Mike Johnson, Writer
PWInsider.com

CAPSTONE PRESS
a capstone imprint

Velocity is published by Capstone Press,
1710 Roe Crest Drive, North Mankato, Minnesota 56003.
www.capstonepub.com

Library of Congress Cataloging-in-Publication Data
Skog, Jason.
Kurt Angle : from Olympian to wrestling machine / by Jason Skog.
p. cm.—(Velocity. Pro wrestling stars)
Includes bibliographical references and index.
Summary: "Describes the life of Kurt Angle, both in and out of the ring"—Provided
by publisher.
ISBN 978-1-4296-8682-2 (library binding)
ISBN 978-1-62065-360-9 (ebook pdf)
1. Angle, Kurt—Juvenile literature. 2. Wrestlers—United States—Biography—Juvenile
literature. I. Title.
GV1196.A55S56 2013
796.72092—dc23 [B]   2012011303

Editorial Credits

Mandy Robbins, editor; Sarah Bennett, designer; Laura Manthe, production specialist

Photo Credits

Art Parts: Ron and Joe, Inc., 40 (fork), 41 (superhero); Corbis: Retna Ltd./Joe Stevens, 45,
Sygma/Gainsanti-Langevin-Orban, 9; Getty Images: Sports Illustrated/George Tiedemann,
6, WireImage/KMazur, 23, WireImage/Theo Wargo, 24; Globe Photos: John Barrett, 37;
iStockphotos: grimgram, 30-31 (boxing ring), inktycoon, 44 (wrestlers), james steidl, 28-29
(boxing ring), Kayann Legg, 5 (wrestlers); Newscom: WENN Photos DM2, 19, ZUMA Press,
32, 39, 40, ZUMA Press/Globe Photos, 11, ZUMA Press/Mary Ann Owen, 17, ZUMA Press/
Milan Ryba, 13, 27, ZUMA Press/UPN-TV/WWF, 4, 18, ZUMAPress/Globe Photos/John
Barrett, cover; Photo by Wrealano@aol.com, 15; Shutterstock: Africa Studio, 44 (medals),
Anastasios Kandris, 29 (belt), astudio, 38 (stamp), buriy, 14 (background), CLIPAREA/
Custom Media, 36, doodle, 7 (whistle), Featureflash, 21, GraphicGeoff, 43 (fighter),
Lightspring, 35, lozas, 41 (menu), maryo, 20-21 (Earth), Master3D, 44-45 (road), mmaxer,
9 (medal), Moneca, 8-9 (stars and stripes), mutation, 33, Rudy Balasko, 4-5 (Pittsburgh
background), SFerdon, 43 (punch, knockout); The Kobal Collection: Solaris, 42; Wikimedia:
Fatima, cover, 1 (background), Peepzilla, 34, Robertlbeukema, 29 (inset)

Artistic Effects

Shutterstock

Printed in the United States of America in Stevens Point, Wisconsin.
032012   006678WZF12

TABLE OF CONTENTS

CHAPTER 1

A WRESTLER
LONG BEFORE PRO WRESTLING

Some fans love him, and some fans love to hate him. But either way, Kurt Angle is one of the greatest wrestlers of all time. He has earned multiple college titles, an Olympic gold medal, and many pro wrestling titles. Kurt's accomplishments in **amateur** wrestling and in the professional ring have made him a legend.

amateur—describes a sports league that athletes take part in for pleasure rather than for money

Kurt was born in Pittsburgh, Pennsylvania. He began wrestling at age 6. Even at that young age, Kurt showed athletic potential. He had speed, strength, and determination. Kurt was the youngest of six children. He had four very athletic brothers. Kurt first learned to wrestle at home with them. Later in his career his brothers were always ringside, offering encouragement and advice.

As a child, Kurt was extremely competitive. When he lost a match, he often cried because he wanted to win so badly.

When Kurt was just 16, his father died in a construction accident. Kurt's mother continued to support Kurt's wrestling after his dad's death. She drove him to practices and matches and cheered him on from the stands.

5

WRESTLER ON THE RISE

When Kurt entered high school, his reputation as an athlete was well known. He played football, baseball, and basketball. But his ability on the wrestling mat attracted the most attention. Kurt went undefeated his freshman year. Kurt qualified for the state tournament as a sophomore. He placed third at the state championships as a junior. When he was a senior, Kurt won the 1987 Pennsylvania state wrestling championship.

Kurt celebrated after defeating North Carolina State's Sylvester Terkay to win the 1992 NCAA Championships.

College wrestling teams were eager to **recruit** Kurt to wrestle for them. Kurt decided to wrestle for Pennsylvania's Clarion University in the demanding heavyweight division. At 208 pounds (94 kilograms), Kurt was small for a heavyweight wrestler. But he didn't let his size hold him back. Kurt went on to win two Division I national titles and was a three-time **All-American**.

There are two ways to win a wrestling match: score more points than your opponent or pin him or her to the mat. These are the rules of amateur wrestling:

PIN

A pin or "fall" is when you put your opponent on the mat with both shoulders or shoulder blades in contact with the mat for two seconds.

HOW TO SCORE POINTS:

TAKEDOWN

You score two points for taking your opponent down to the mat and controlling him.

ESCAPE

You score one point for getting away, or escaping, if your opponent has you down on the mat.

REVERSAL

You score two points if your opponent has you down on the mat and you are able to gain control of your opponent.

NEAR FALL

You get two or three points if you almost—but not entirely—are able to pin your opponent.

PENALTY POINTS

Your opponent may be awarded penalty points if you use an illegal hold or commit any of a number of technical violations.

RIDING TIME

In college wrestling, athletes can score points for controlling their opponents for a certain length of time.

recruit—to ask someone to join a company or an organization

All-American—a college athlete who is considered one of the best in his or her sport in a particular year

OLYMPIC HERO

Kurt launched to national fame during the 1996 Olympic Games in Atlanta, Georgia. Kurt had trained hard for the Olympics. His eight-hour workouts included practice matches against other wrestlers, a difficult weight-lifting routine, and 200-yard (183-meter) sprints uphill. By the time he reached the Olympic mat, Kurt was stronger than he'd ever been. His only concern was a neck injury that he had suffered at the Olympic trials. But Kurt was determined to wrestle through the pain.

Once he got to the Olympics, Kurt wrestled his way to the championship match. He was set to wrestle the highly **favored** Iranian wrestler, Abbas Jadidi.

Kurt and Jadidi wrestled an intense match. It lasted a full eight minutes and ended with a score of one to one. The judge's panel was forced to pick a winner.

The judges discussed the match and told the referee their decision. The referee raised Kurt's hand in victory. Kurt hugged him and dropped to his knees in tears.

American fans erupted in applause. Kurt was swarmed by photographers and reporters asking him about his unexpected victory.

favored—when a person is expected to win

Kurt wept tears of joy after winning the gold medal at the 1996 Summer Olympics in Atlanta.

IN KURT'S OWN WORDS

"Finally, after I posed for all the pictures and the press conference ended, I took my gold medal off and put it around my mom's neck. I wanted her to have it for everything she'd done for me," he said.

Later on, when the frenzy died down, Kurt found his mother. He put his Olympic gold medal around her neck.

CHAPTER 2
ENTERING PRO WRESTLING

The glow of Kurt's Olympic gold medal was still warm when he became interested in professional wrestling. Kurt wasn't entirely sold on it at first. He worked briefly as a sports reporter for a local Pittsburgh TV station. He also tried out for the NFL's Pittsburgh Steelers football team, but they turned him down.

On October 26, 1996, Kurt's first taste of pro wrestling came at a match hosted by Extreme Championship Wrestling (ECW). Kurt served as a commentator. In October 1998 Kurt attended a pro wrestling training camp for World Wrestling Federation (WWF). His athletic skill and bold personality made him a great fit for pro wrestling. WWF officials were impressed by Kurt. They had him lined up for a match just three days after showing up at camp. It was the beginning of a promising career.

OCTOBER 26, 1996

Kurt served as a commentator at a match hosted by ECW.

OCTOBER 1998

Kurt attended a WWF wrestling training and tryout camp. Three days later, he was in his first match, an untelevised bout against Christian Cage.

MARCH 7, 1999

Kurt appeared on WWF's *Sunday Night Heat* in a stunt with Tiger Ali Singh. Singh paid Kurt to blow his nose on the American flag. Kurt instead blew his nose on Singh's flag and got into a scuffle with him.

NOVEMBER 14, 1999

Kurt made his in-ring TV **debut**, defeating Shawn Stasiak.

FEBRUARY 8, 2000

Kurt won the WWF European Championship, defeating Val Venis.

FEBRUARY 27, 2000

Kurt won the WWF Intercontinental Championship, defeating Chris Jericho. He became the first wrestler to hold this title and the WWF European Championship at the same time.

OCTOBER 22, 2000

Kurt defeated The Rock to become WWF Champion for the first time.

FACT

In 2002 the WWF changed its name to World Wrestling Entertainment (WWE) to avoid a lawsuit. The letters "WWF" were alread associated with another organization, the World Wildlife Fund.

debut—a person's first public appearance

GOOD GOES BAD

In Kurt's early days as a pro wrestler, he played a **babyface**. Kurt presented himself as an American hero. He wore a **replica** of his Olympic gold medal and a red, white, and blue uniform. But Kurt found it easier to excite the audience if they were rooting against him. After he lost his championship belts in April 2000, Kurt dropped the hero image and turned **heel**.

It was Kurt's match against fan-favorite The Rock in October 2000 that solidified his image as a heel. Kurt laid his bad attitude on thick. After a long and brutal match, Kurt defeated The Rock. He was hated by fans everywhere—and he loved it.

IN KURT'S OWN WORDS

"I've always enjoyed playing the heel," Kurt said. "I enjoyed it even more since they made me a little nastier after I lost the [Intercontinental Championship] belt."

JULY 24, 2001

Kurt defeated Booker T to take the World Championship Wrestling (WCW) World Championship.

SEPTEMBER 23, 2001

Kurt defeated Steve Austin to become WWF World Champion.

OCTOBER 22, 2001

Kurt won the WCW U.S. Championship against Rhyno on *Raw*.

DECEMBER 15, 2002

Kurt beat Big Show to win the WWE Championship.

JULY 27, 2003

Kurt defeated Big Show and Brock Lesnar to win the WWE Championship.

JANUARY 10, 2006

Kurt won *SmackDown Battle Royal* to become the WWE World Heavyweight Champion.

MAY 13, 2007

Kurt defeated Sting and Total Nonstop Action (TNA) World Champion Christian Cage to become the new TNA World Champion.

JUNE 21, 2009

Kurt won the TNA World Heavyweight Championship title in a King of the Mountain match.

AUGUST 7, 2011

Kurt beat Sting to win TNA's World Heavyweight Championship.

babyface—a wrestler who acts as a hero in the ring

replica—an exact copy of something

heel—a wrestler who acts as a villain in the ring

CHAPTER 3
ROCKING
INTO THE RING

When Kurt's entrance music starts pumping, the crowd roars, and fans jump to their feet. Certain songs serve as familiar sound tracks when wrestlers strut their stuff into the ring. Kurt has announced his arrival in the ring with a handful of signature songs.

For the first seven years of his pro wrestling career, Kurt entered to the song "Medal" by Jim Johnston. When the audience heard the song begin, that was their cue to start booing.

"Medal" was later replaced by another song written by Jim Johnston. This song was Kurt's response to an insult from pro wrestler Edge.

More recently Kurt has entered to "Gold Medal," by Tha Trademarc. "Gold Medal" is a reference to the 1996 Olympic gold medal Kurt won.

Kurt has also had a number of nicknames throughout his career. Most of them had to do with his Olympic past. Others recognized his athleticism and many championship titles. Among them are:

YOUR OLYMPIC HERO

THE GODFATHER OF THE MAIN EVENT MAFIA

THE AMERICAN HERO

THE WRESTLING MACHINE

CHAPTER 4

KURT'S BIG MOVES

Few pro wrestlers have as many **signature moves** as Kurt does. His time as an amateur wrestler served him well. He is able to move quickly across the ring and use a number of moves to disable or defeat his opponents. Some of his favorite moves include:

DOUBLE-LEG TAKEDOWN

Kurt grabs an opponent's legs or waist. He throws him off balance and tosses him to the mat

EUROPEAN UPPERCUT

Kurt drives his forearm up and under an opponent's chin or into his face.

HEAD BUTT

Kurt transforms his large head into a weapon. He drives it into an opponent's body to deliver a punishing blow.

MOONSAULT

The Moonsault may be one of the flashiest moves in pro wrestling. First Kurt climbs to the top rope. He faces away from his opponent, who is down on the mat. Then Kurt flips backward, landing on top of his opponent.

REAR NAKED CHOKEHOLD

Kurt gets behind his opponent. He wraps his arm around his opponent's neck and grabs his own **biceps**.

GERMAN SUPLEX

Kurt stands behind his opponent and wraps his arms around the opponent's waist. Kurt then lifts the other wrestler over his shoulder and falls backward. This movement slams the opponent's head and shoulders into the mat.

signature move—the move for which a wrestler is best known; this move is also called a finishing move

biceps—the large muscle on the front of your arm between your shoulder and inner elbow

FINISH 'EM OFF!

When it's time to finish a match, Kurt knows how to get the job done. These are two of his favorite match-ending signature moves.

ANGLE SLAM

If he wants to be sure his opponent is finished, Kurt pulls off the Angle Slam. Kurt hoists an opponent up onto his shoulders like he's doing a fireman's carry. With a quick swing of his shoulders and a boost of his arms, Kurt lifts his opponent high into the air. His opponent is vertical for a brief moment. Then Kurt sends him smashing to the floor, either face-first or flat on his back. After that, it's all over. Kurt needs only to hold him down for the final 1-2-3 count.

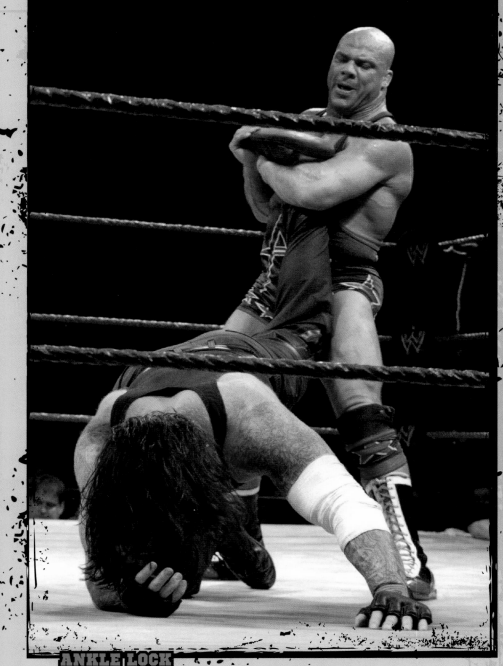

ANKLE LOCK

If his opponent is still showing signs of life, Kurt can opt for an ankle lock. Kurt grabs his opponent's ankle and begins twisting it in painful ways. Eventually, Kurt's opponents usually "tap out." This is the sign to the referee that a wrestler has had enough and is ready to give up. It's rare for any of Kurt's opponents to escape the dreaded ankle lock.

CHAPTER 5
FAMOUS FEUDS

As Kurt's popularity grew, his **feuds** with fellow wrestlers became legendary. Kurt would often win a match against one of the big-name stars and then lose to him in a rematch.

Kurt's heel image helped him make enemies easily. He attracted the scorn of some of the biggest names in the business. For a long time, it seemed, it was Kurt against the world.

RANDY ORTON
Height: 6 ft, 5 in (196 cm)
Weight: 235 lb (107 kg)

THE ROCK
Height: 6 ft, 5 in (196 cm)
Weight: 260 lb (118 kg)

CHRISTIAN
Height: 6 ft, 1 in (185 cm)
Weight: 212 lb (96 kg)

TRIPLE H
Height: 6 ft, 4 in (193 cm)
Weight: 255 lb (116 kg)

UNDERTAKER
Height: 6 ft, 10 in (208 cm)
Weight: 299 lb (136 kg)

STEVE AUSTIN
Height: 6 ft, 2 in (188 cm)
Weight: 252 lb (114 kg)

feud—a long-running quarrel between two people or groups of people

CHRIS JERICHO
Height: 6 ft (183 cm)
Weight: 226 lb (103 kg)

JOHN CENA
Height: 6 ft, 1 in (185 cm)
Weight: 251 lb (114 kg)

RIC FLAIR
Height: 6 ft, 1 in (185 cm)
Weight: 243 lb (110 kg)

BIG SHOW
Height: 7 ft (213 cm)
Weight: 441 lb (200 kg)

HULK HOGAN
Height: 6 ft, 7 in (201 cm)
Weight: 303 lb (137 kg)

KANE
Height: 7 ft (213 cm)
Weight: 323 lb (147 kg)

RIKISHI
Height: 6 ft, 1 in (185 cm)
Weight: 425 lb (193 kg)

EDDIE GUERRERO
Height: 5 ft, 8 in (173 cm)
Weight: 220 lb (100 kg)

THE CLASH OF KURT AND EDDIE

One of the first wrestlers to get into repeated tangles with Kurt was Eddie Guerrero. Eddie was one of the fans' favorite wrestlers. When he went up against Kurt, the crowd was always on Eddie's side. The rivalry reached a high point when they squared off for the WWE Championship at *Wrestlemania* in 2004.

Kurt and Eddie had a number of tense encounters prior to the match. When fight night arrived, the crowd was primed for a good show. They got it.

The match lasted nearly 20 minutes. The two men went back and forth with no clear winner. With Eddie in an Ankle Lock, Kurt seemed ready to win. But Eddie escaped. Eddie also had a trick up his sleeve—or at least up his boot. At one point in the match, Eddie pretended his foot was injured and loosened the laces on his boot.

EDDIE GUERRERO

HEIGHT
5 ft, 8 in (173 cm)

WEIGHT
220 lb (100 kg)

SIGNATURE MOVES
Frog Splash, Lasso from El Paso

Later in the match Kurt put Eddie in the dreaded Ankle Lock again. This time Eddie slipped out of his boot and escaped the hold. A confused Kurt stood holding an empty boot, and Eddie pounced on him. Moments later he had Kurt pinned for the win.

The two men continued their feud, leading to a number of memorable matches. The high-quality wrestling and chemistry between Kurt and Eddie made for a memorable feud. Many fans think the feud between Kurt and Eddie is among pro wrestling's all-time greatest rivalries.

KURT VS. BROCK LESNAR

Kurt and Brock Lesnar were both accomplished amateur wrestlers before turning pro. Perhaps that's what made their feud so memorable. The two men battled for the WWE Championship. Kurt won it in December 2002. But he wouldn't have won it without the help he received from Lesnar. Soon after, Lesnar decided he wanted the title for himself.

BROCK LESNAR

HEIGHT
6 ft, 3 in (191 cm)

WEIGHT
265 lbs (120 kg)

SIGNATURE MOVES
F-5, Shooting Star Press First

Brock Lesnar and Kurt Angle posed with the WWE Championship belt before facing off at *WrestleMania* on March 18, 2003.

In March 2003 the two men faced off during an episode of *SmackDown!* If Lesnar won, he would take Kurt's WWE title belt. But Kurt tricked Lesnar by pulling a switcheroo. Kurt's brother Eric looks a lot like him. Before the match, Eric took Kurt's place in the ring when the lights were out. Lesnar almost had Eric pinned when he realized Eric wasn't Kurt. Lesnar charged offstage looking for Kurt, and Kurt switched places with Eric again. When Lesnar came back to finish Eric off, Kurt pinned Lesnar. Through this trickery, Kurt kept the WWE title.

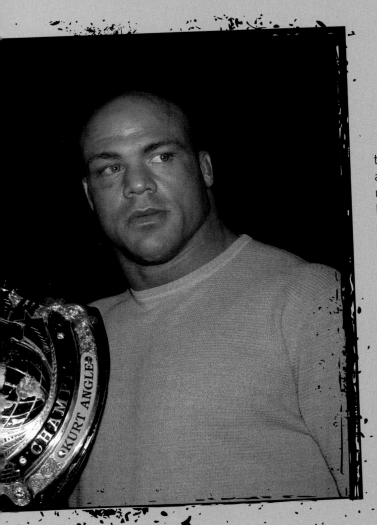

Later that month the bitter rivals met up at *WrestleMania*. In the main event, Lesnar and Kurt went back and forth until Kurt had Lesnar in an Ankle Lock. Lesnar managed to escape, but Kurt tried to do the Angle Slam. Lesnar came back with an F-5. To do this move, Lesnar lifted Kurt over his shoulders and slammed him face-first into the mat.

Then Lesnar climbed to the top rope so he could smash into Kurt and finish him off. But Kurt rolled out of the way! Lesnar laid stunned on the canvas, giving Kurt an opportunity to win. Kurt tried to pick up Lesnar, but it was not to be. In a flash, Lesnar hit him with another F-5. Kurt was pinned, and Brock Lesnar was the WWE Champion.

A MATCH FOR THE AGES

Kurt and Shawn Michaels spent months feuding, which led up to *Wrestlemania* on April 3, 2005. This match is considered one of the most incredible matches in pro wrestling history. When the men entered the ring at the Staples Center in Los Angeles, fan excitement was at an all-time high.

Kurt and Michaels went back and forth in a match that lasted nearly 30 minutes. At one point, Michaels jumped from the top rope and drove his elbow into Kurt's chest. It was a punishing blow. Kurt seemed to be down for the count. But moments later, he staggered up from the mat. Michaels attempted to deliver a finishing kick to Kurt. Kurt responded by grabbing Michaels' leg and twisting his ankle into an Ankle Lock. Michaels escaped by grabbing onto the lower rope of the ring.

As the two men continued the match, it was still unclear who would be victorious. At one point, both men were flat on their backs, exhausted. As Michaels struggled to his feet, Kurt reached out and grabbed hold of his ankle. Again, he applied his dreaded Ankle Lock. After minutes of struggling, Michaels finally tapped out.

SHAWN MICHAELS

HEIGHT
6 ft, 1 in (185 cm)

WEIGHT
225 lbs (102 kg)

NICKNAMES
Heartbreak Kid, HBK

SIGNATURE MOVE
Sweet Chin Music

FACT

During his feud with Shawn Michaels, Kurt bragged that he accomplished in weeks what it took years for Michaels to do.

CHAPTER 6

A TRUE CHAMPION

Kurt Angle is one of the most successful contenders in pro wrestling history. He's the only wrestler to win every individual title in his first year as a pro. In 2006 and 2007, fans voted Kurt one of the world's greatest pro wrestlers of all time.

In October 2011 Kurt was inducted into the George Tragos/Lou Thesz Professional Wrestling Hall of Fame in Waterloo, Iowa. This honor is for wrestlers who have made a big impact on pro wrestling. They must also have a strong amateur wrestling background.

FACT

Kurt is a 12-time World Heavyweight Champion.

KURT'S BIG WINS

KURT HAS WON:

★ all of the TNA and WWE Championships

★ TNA's Division X Championship

★ the WCW Championship, Intercontinental Championship, European Championship, Hardcore Championship, and King of the Ring title

Kurt Angle shows off his championship belts at TNA Impact in 2007.

KURT'S PRO WRESTLING RECORD (AS OF 2011):
331 WINS
256 LOSSES
45 DRAWS

KURT'S BIGGEST CHAMPIONSHIP BOUTS

When it comes to championship bouts, Kurt always steps up his game. He has faced some of wrestling's most fearsome opponents. And whether he wins or loses, Kurt always delivers an entertaining, athletic, and emotional match. His most dramatic matches include:

OCTOBER 22, 2000

Kurt beat out The Rock to win at *No Mercy* with the help of Rikishi. Rikishi had been trying to help The Rock by kicking Kurt. Instead, Rikishi missed Kurt and kicked The Rock. Angle then knocked The Rock out cold with the Angle Slam. It was Kurt's first WWF Championship win.

DECEMBER 15, 2002

Kurt defeated Big Show at *Armageddon*. Kurt battled back from an early takedown and got Big Show in a sleeper hold. But Big Show reversed the hold and flipped Kurt to the mat. In the end, Kurt got some helpful interference from Brock Lesnar. Lesnar lifted Big Show and slammed him to the mat, allowing Kurt to pin Big Show for the win.

JULY 27, 2003

Kurt unseated defending champ Brock Lesnar at *Vengeance*. In a triple-threat match between Kurt, Lesnar, and Big Show, Kurt came out on top. In the end, he used the Angle Slam to take out Big Show. He then used the same move on Lesnar to set him up for the pin.

JANUARY 10, 2006

Kurt won the WWE Championship in a Battle Royal match against an army of 20 other wrestlers.

MAY 13, 2007

Kurt beat Sting and NWA Champion Christian Cage in a three-way match. At the end, Kurt put Sting in an Ankle Lock just as Sting had Cage pinned. Kurt then pinned Sting in order to beat them both. He was the new NWA Champion.

AUGUST 7, 2011

Kurt defeated Sting during *HardCORE Justice*. Before the match Kurt had promised fans one of the most exciting matches they would ever see. The long contest saw injuries to both wrestlers. The brutal back-and-forth match left both men exhausted on the mat near the end. As they struggled to get up, Hulk Hogan entered the arena with a folding chair. Hogan was about to hit Sting with the chair when Kurt stirred to life. Kurt grabbed the chair out of Hogan's hands and struck Sting with it himself. Kurt picked up a dazed Sting up over his shoulders. He performed the Angle Slam, smashing Sting to the mat and pinning him for the win.

CHAPTER 7
SWITCHING STAGES

Kurt appeared in some of WWE's biggest matches on the sport's biggest stages. He wrestled on *WrestleMania*, *King of the Ring*, *Smackdown!*, and *Raw*. Audiences couldn't get enough of Kurt. But the wear and tear of the busy WWE schedule was taking a toll on his body. Kurt suffered several injuries and didn't have time to recover properly before getting back in the ring.

Kurt Angle tangles with Desmond Wolf on the TNA Wrestling Tour in 2010.

TNA vs. WWE

In 2001 the WWE was the only nationally televised wrestling program on TV. Pro wrestling father-and-son duo Jerry and Jeff Jarrett decided WWE could use some competition. In 2002 they founded TNA Wrestling. Today TNA attracts more than 1 million viewers each week to its wrestling programs. Kurt has become one of the company's biggest stars. WWE's weekly program draws almost 3 million viewers. But it's safe to say that TNA has become a serious competitor.

In 2006 Kurt left WWE for a lighter schedule at TNA Wrestling. There Kurt wrestled on *No Surrender, iMPACT,* and *Against All Odds.* TNA has a smaller following than WWE. But Kurt still has a lot of appeal with fans.

In Kurt's own Words

"The future at TNA is wrestling, wrestling, wrestling, wrestling. I've signed a new three-year deal with TNA. The rumor was I was going back to WWE, but that's not happening. I'm staying here until I retire."

33

CHAPTER 8
INJURIES AND AILMENTS

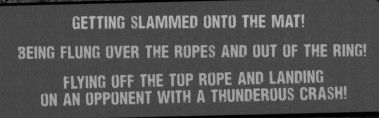

GETTING SLAMMED ONTO THE MAT!

BEING FLUNG OVER THE ROPES AND OUT OF THE RING!

FLYING OFF THE TOP ROPE AND LANDING
ON AN OPPONENT WITH A THUNDEROUS CRASH!

There are dozens of moves in pro wrestling—all of which pose danger to the wrestlers if performed incorrectly. Even when things go according to plan, wrestling causes extreme wear and tear on the body.

Kurt knows about wrestling injuries all too well. Throughout his career, he has battled many injuries. Some of them have been serious enough to threaten to end Kurt's career. Yet he has worked hard to perform night after night, regardless of injuries. These are some of the injuries Kurt has suffered during his time in the ring:

NECK

Over the course of his career, Kurt has broken several **vertebrae**. Eventually, he had a surgery on them called surgical fusion.

RIBS

Kurt dislocated his ribs on October 10, 2010, in a three-man match with Jeff Hardy and Mr. Anderson.

ABDOMINAL

On August 13, 2006, Kurt suffered a torn abdominal muscle in a loss to Rob Van Dam.

HAMSTRING

Kurt strained his hamstring during *WrestleMania* on March 30, 2003, in his match against Brock Lesnar.

vertebrae—the small bones that surround and protect the spinal cord

PAIN IN THE NECK

Kurt's neck has been a source of pain, frustration, and concern for much of his career. Just before the 1996 Olympics, Kurt suffered from two cracked vertebrae. Still, he pressed on. With the help of pain medication, Kurt was able to earn his gold medal.

Kurt's neck problems re-emerged later on in his career. By April 2003 Kurt needed major surgery to repair years of damage.

Kurt enlisted the help of surgeon Dr. Hae-Dong Jho to fix his neck. But rather than a more common surgery that takes longer to heal, Kurt chose a different approach. As a result of this newer surgery, Kurt was able to return to wrestling fairly quickly. In fact, he was itching to get back in the ring just two weeks after surgery. But WWE officials weren't going to let him do that without approval from his doctors.

Kurt spent countless hours doing exercises to regain strength in his neck. Usually recovering from neck surgery requires a year of **rehabilitation**. For Kurt, it took just two months to get back in shape.

By June 2003 Kurt had returned to the wrestling world. He appeared at WWE events but he didn't fight in the ring. However, soon afterward, his doctors said he was ready to wrestle. Kurt jumped in the ring on July 27, 2003, against Brock Lesnar and Big Show in a three-man match at *Vengeance*. Kurt beat them both and regained the WWE Championship. The surgery had been a success—Kurt Angle was back.

Despite Big Show's power, Kurt was able to beat both him and Brock Lesnar in his WWE comeback after neck surgery.

rehabilitation—therapy that helps people recover their health or abilities

CHAPTER 9

LIFE OUTSIDE THE RING

Kurt has become one of pro wrestling's biggest stars. But he's not just famous for his skills inside the ring. Kurt's exciting personality and wrestling success have led to appearances on TV and movie roles.

Kurt has appeared on a number of talk shows. They include *The Tonight Show with Jay Leno* and *Late Night with Conan O'Brien*. Kurt has also appeared on *Live with Regis and Kathie Lee* and the *Today* show. He's also been on ESPN's *Cold Pizza*, MTV's *Made*, and ABC's *Extreme Makeover: Home Edition*.

HOLLYWOOD

Kurt has even appeared in several independent films. He has played a wrestler, a prison inmate, a coach, an FBI agent, and a sheriff. Kurt has said that he would like to pursue acting more seriously when his wrestling days are over.

In 2011 Kurt appeared in a movie called *Warrior*. Kurt played a fierce Russian mixed martial arts (MMA) fighter named Koba. He said the role required him to be singularly focused on his opponent. The result was a menacing character fans loved.

Director Bruce Koehler gives Kurt direction while filming the 2010 movie *Death from Above*.

FIGHTING FOR HEALTHY FOOD

Wrestlers have to stay in good shape. Because of this, Kurt has always made fitness and nutrition a top priority. To help others eat healthy and stay in shape, Kurt has developed Angle Foods. This line of ready-made meals includes dishes that are high in fiber, protein, and vegetables. These meals are good for building muscle and staying lean.

IN KURT'S OWN WORDS

"Diet represents 80 percent of our fitness goals and results," Kurt says.

Kurt came up with the idea when he was on the road traveling between wrestling matches. He knows how hard it can be to cook healthy meals when people are busy. Kurt's slogan for Angle Foods is "Heat. Eat. Go." Kurt sells his meals online and in grocery stores.

menu

Kurt's signature dishes include:

Chicken and Vegetables with Rice

Salmon and Broccoli

Shrimp and Vegetables

High-Fiber Cheese Pizza

MMA FOR KURT?

Outside of wrestling, Kurt has explored other areas where he could apply his athletic skills. He has always had an interest in MMA fighting. Kurt considered entering MMA right after college, but he decided on wrestling instead.

Kurt received a look inside the world of MMA while he was preparing for his role in the movie *Warrior*. The role required Kurt to spend three months in MMA training.

Kurt pummels his opponent in the movie *Warrior*.

"It [the movie] was a lot of fun and if I wanted to go into MMA, I learned a lot just from that movie alone.

PUNCH!!

Kurt has talked with some of MMA's top organizers and officials. So far, they haven't reached any agreements. There are concerns that Kurt wouldn't pass the medical exams because he has broken his neck five times. But Kurt says he feels better than ever and is still interested in MMA.

KNOCKOUT!!

THE ROAD AHEAD

Kurt had planned to return to the Olympic Games in London in 2012. He spent a year training for the Olympic tryouts, called trials. But the week before the Olympic trials, he suffered a devastating knee injury. Kurt was forced to withdraw his bid for the Olympics.

Kurt was disappointed to give up his Olympic dreams. But he has other ways to keep busy. Kurt plans to improve his acting skills and also focus on pro wrestling. For now, he remains a top wrestler with TNA. Kurt continues to show that he still has what it takes to stay at the top of pro wrestling. In 2011 he held the TNA Heavyweight title.

IN KURT'S OWN WORDS

"In amateur wrestling, I have no control over what's going to happen to me. My No. 1 priority is TNA Wrestling. With TNA, I can work around my injuries and still have a five-star match."

No matter what the future holds for Kurt, he's come a long way from wrestling with his brothers on the living room floor. Today Kurt has a solid reputation as one of the most accomplished amateur and pro wrestlers of all time.

GLOSSARY

All-American (ALL-uh-MARE-uh-kuhn)—a college athlete who is considered one of the best in his or her sport in a particular year

amateur (AM-uh-chur)—describes a sports league that athletes take part in for pleasure rather than for money

babyface (BAY-bee-fayss)—a wrestler who acts as a hero in the ring

biceps (BYE-seps)—the large muscle on the front of your arm between your shoulder and inner elbow

debut (day-BYOO)—a person's first public appearance

favored (FAY-vuhrd)—when a person is expected to win

feud (FYOOD)—a long-running quarrel between two people or groups of people

heel (HEEL)—a wrestler who acts as a villain in the ring

recruit (ri-KROOT)—to ask someone to join a company or an organization

rehabilitation (ree-huh-bil-uh-TAY-shun)—therapy that helps people recover their health or abilities

replica (REP-luh-kuh)—an exact copy of something

signature move (SIG-nuh-chur MOOV)—the move for which a wrestler is best known; this move is also called a finishing move

vertebrae (VUR-tuh-bray)—the small bones that surround and protect the spinal cord

READ MORE

Kaelberer, Angie Peterson. *The Fabulous, Freaky, Unusual History of Pro Wrestling.* Unusual Histories. North Mankato, Minn.: Capstone Press, 2011.

Middleton, Haydn. *Modern Olympic Games.* The Olympics. Chicago: Heinemann Library, 2008.

Nemeth, Jason D. *Kurt Angle.* Stars of Pro Wrestling. North Mankato, Minn.: Capstone Press, 2010.

INTERNET SITES

FactHound offers a safe, fun way to find Internet sites related to this book. All of the sites on FactHound have been researched by our staff.

Here's all you do:

Visit *www.facthound.com*

Enter this code: 9781429686822

INDEX

31/32